HALCYON TIME

Books by Hugh Hennedy

Criticism
Unity in Barsetshire

Poetry
Old Winchester Hill
Halcyon Time

HALCYON TIME

Hugh Hennedy

Oyster River Press

ISBN 1 882291 54 9

Cover art and drawings by Charles Chu

Acknowledgments are due to the editors
of the following publications where some
of these poems appeared for the first time:
*Ball State University Forum, Folio of
Maine Poets & Writers...1980, Kennebec,
Tar River Poetry, Tight.*

O y s t e r   R i v e r   P r e s s
20 Riverview Rd   Durham   NH   03824

SEEING MOVING THINGS

Though outside it is still winter, old snow
Being still on the ground, the maple tree
And the bushes beyond came this morning
Not long after dawning alive with birds!

First in the bare tree there appeared what seemed
Nearly the perfection of a blue bird;
Seconds later, the first one having flown,
A bird so small I named it warbeler,

While concurrently the bushes were in-
Habited, bushily flowing now with
Flitterings too reeling far away for
Any sure sign of denomination,

Though one or two might have worn crests of jay.
Were there really in my maple in Maine
Still held in winter blue bird and warbler
Or was there but one of uncertain kind

Seen in different ways? The warbeler,
I now conclude as now I see outside
No birds, nothing but bushes, maple, snow,
Was no more certainly sighted than spelled.

Despite inadequacies of spelling,
Sighting, because of all the vagaries
Of birds and the persistency of snow,
Those birds, those seeing moving things, were seen
Early today not indifferently.

For Valjeane

CONTENTS

AT SUMMER'S END

Woolly mammoths of the lowtide shore
Huddle quietly together while
The ocean beyond snorts and rumbles
And shuffles and most of the gulls stand
Almost as still as pooledwater

BEFORE ANOTHER FIRST CLASS

Goldenrod and rosehips and roses
And batons of grass growing through
And ocean down below beating the time
And somewhere up above
A crow getting into the act

SEEN IN SEPTEMBER

Standing on the rock,
Reflecting in the pool,
The one gull
Preens and preens
In the early light.

Standing on the rock
Blocking reflection,
The other gull
Stands and stands
In another light.

SEPTEMBER UNIVERSITY

Sparrows in and out of
Light fly and stand on
The bathed campus

               the knee

Of a visitor creaking
In and out of socket

BEFORE THE FAMILY REUNION

Where once the blackbirds were
And where they will be again
Grass and reeds and bushes
Almost do not stir

In absence of the blacks
Their browns and central grays
Still from light to dark
Move almost unmoving

FALL MIGRATION

After seeing
From the mountain
Hawks sailing over
The White Mountains,
Green in the west,
And the green ocean,
Blue in the east —
Blue and smudged
By an island
Or two and dotted
By the white of sails —
He saw from sleep
An island brightly lit
Where before was smudge
And he heard a voice — his own —
Say, he thinks, Aruba.

ONE AND ALL

The thing about the Canada goose
In the water is you can see it swim.
It, unlike the duck and the swan,
Lets you see it pump and pump and pump.

How delightful this lack of
Artfulness, this rendering
Of feet by neck, this
Revealing of impulse, doing of the work!

AFTER THE ARRIVAL OF ACE

Now that he has arrived and scattered
At the side of the road his crumbs
The birds are still strangely quiet.

They scurry around and flip larger
Pieces up almost as
If for tap-off, but if contests

Take place, there is no roar of crowd,
No panting nor grunting to be heard,
Only when an engine grinds close, the slap

Of wings ascending leaving the quiet
Roadside to the cat coiled
Behind the tree, the pigeons being

Quiet again on the roof behind,
The sun warm on napes of watchers.

DOWN ACROSS THE ALLEY

That fluffing of the wings,
He suddenly understood,
Has nothing to do with grooming,
Everything with dying.

That poor pigeon
Labors, muddied down there
Now in the puddle, to
Put out the guttering light.

ALSO FOR MIGUEL

As the feathering gull drops his prised shells
And catches them still in the air, spears of grass
And clusters of asters quiver in the breeze of the cello.

Ah, that old enchanter is at it again.

AND THE KINGFISHER AFTER

Sticking close to
each other until
they get back close to
shore where they move out
spread into reeds from which
emerging the wood ducks
close up rank again
brightly painted soldiers
glued and unglued on the pond

CLEANSING THE DOORS
AFTER HAGGLING

Looking headon
In front of waving
Grass not much
Less tall than it
Rather like
A small ostrich
At an edge of the mill pond
The great blue
Heron renews
Its heronhood
When it turns its dagger
Head to aim it
At an alighted
Dove or to sight
Me better
Rooted at the curb
Much less still
Than any heron

And that crook
In the neck when it
Takes off it
Too it renews

ON FRANCIS'S AND GUY'S DAY

Billowing the weeds brown on the surface,
Lifting up and setting down
The several gulls riding in the weeds
And at their edges, the waves slide in
While spears of grass and clusters of asters
Quiver and arc on shore in the breeze.

DRESS OF GRAY MORNING

White lace settling on rocks
And rolling in out there

Brown lace moving in air
On a fringe of the pond in here

And crows selving in the wind

AFTER THE ONE AND THE OTHER

After the flicker came in
Black over the waves
Before assuming with closeness
Color and form and winging
Yellow and white and buff to a tree

And after the crow went
Black all the way
Across the ruby-smooth surface
Of the pond the long-tailed sparrow
Appeared in the bush and sang out

Over the pond
Dadadada deet
Deet dadadada

AFTER THE ROBINS

The morning seems
not so bleak
the season
not so advanced

But after these days when
so many leaves
have yet to fall
what bleakening

For them
for you
for all

CONCORDE

The cormorant comes in low,
low, low, low, over the waves until
almost at their breaking he
lowers his gear to brake to a stop
outspread wings and slim fuselage up.

Ungainly bird so full of grace
this bright fall morning.

AFTER THE CORMORANT

The wind blows and bushes bend
and I being as dependent on it as

headed into it with wings outspread
the gull above

shining in the water with wings tucked in
the black ducks

as those birds that find thee perfect
like the bufflehead diving in the pond

breathe fresh air

BACK IN STANDARD TIME

The sun bright in the eyes once more
Across the road the bushes
Recently shielding the pond from view
Having now lost their leaves
The blue of water if not of ice
Comes back into sight

While on this side of the road
Mergansers in the cove
Dazzle as smaller birds fly
In and out of sight

AFTER STORM

Gulls in the light
winging white the morning
and a great blue heron
braving it too
cleaving those thin legs
through thin air
from shade to shade

And crow and cormorant
swim the sky in their black suits

But what most takes the eye
the white of gulls
against the blue of sky

ON ELECTION DAY MORNING

The loon and the grebe dive out of the sun
And I in the sun squint at the quickness
Of the grebe, squint at the ease of the loon.

And now with the sun at my back I see
Rocks moving, and I recognize ducks
Absorbing the sun in the still of the sea.

IN GRAY DESPITE BRIGHT
EVELYN NOVEMBER

On the horizon trees
A regular forest wherever
Over the ocean with or
Without the glasses one looks

At last to see Spain
Lying always out there
But who would have imagined
So many trees on that plain

And piercing the skin of the sea
The in-close merganser dives
That skin shivering and shuddering
As if in an ecstasy

IN MID NOVEMBER

How fast the dive of
The female bufflehead!
Flip!

Is she always
Quicker than he?
Flop!

MID-NOVEMBER SIGHTING

Beyond the gulls on the rocks
Ducks way out in swells.

What kind they are too far
To tell, too far to say.

STORM IN NOVEMBER

Off the roiling ocean
Leafstripping wind with rain

Rain snaredrumming within
The gullsustaining wind

AT HARBOUR PLACE IN
CLOUDLESS NOVEMBER

Near the bridge a gull flies like a goose
like a low-flying goose almost

Boats at their tieups stir
and creak and whistle as
the ridged and furrowed river
goes fast to the fecund sea
and pipes of the down drawbridge
play in low register

While in a staff of sun
I stand noting

IN THE SKIM ICE MORNING

In an apparent absence of
Birds, except for an occasional
Gull, standing behind
And above a fringe of tall

Gold grass, cattails,
Like the grass, move
In always present, if not
Always obvious, breeze.

And then, across the way,
Black ducks and mallards drift by
And dabble, drift, dabble, and stand.

OFF THE POOL BEACH IN NOVEMBER

Rosehips in shriveled orange abundance
Blooming on nearly leafless bushes

Lots of oldsquaws showing lots
Of white and lots of upthrust tail

A pair of scoters diving dark
At the inner edge of all that being

BEFORE THANKSGIVING
IN PORTSMOUTH

Some of the gulls slowly drifting
In the center of the pond, two near
An edge stand on themselves, the sun
Shining on them in and on
The drifting water of the Mill Pond.

IN NOVEMBER AFTER ICE

While the gulls flapping and slapping their wings
On the pond and shivering seem restless
Some of them in the air glide
So smooth one wonders why such smoothness
Should bring them down with the rest down there

BEFORE THE THRASHING EIDERS

Not showing a crest that day
the merganser muffled himself
until he dove

Until his quick arcing
mergansered him out of sight
lancelike bill and supine crest

Gorget and spurs and all the rest
quicker than saying
than all

IN A GRAY DECEMBER

A flock of evening grosbeaks
was that morning
skittish by the side of the road

Hungrier or bolder than the males
bearing on each gray shoulder
a yellow smudge
the females returned
after each flight first

Then a mockingbird
and then a dark red smudge
flew across
and then the loon
all alone
was gray and white
in on the graygreen
water of the sea

FROZEN POND MORNING ONE

A pair of buffleheads where one
Expected the loon to be

On a thrust of white a frenzy of wings
And the loon is where the buffleheads were

There where one did
And did not expect him to be

FROZEN POND MORNING TWO

Having cruised through weeds
The merganser dives
As mergansers do,
Arcs herself
From water through air
Into water, her bill
Tracing straight
The circling way,
Plunging down there
Almost faster
Than eye can see,
Surely truer
Than tongue can tell.
At ease apparently
In weeds as well as in
Water and air,
Quicker than a sneeze
She dives, purer
Than circling observers
And sooner complete.

ON THE EVE OF ANOTHER SOLSTICE

Now I no longer have to wonder why
I've been cutting across to the park
by way of the street with the barker
when the next one, dogless, would've
got me there just as fast or faster:
I've been taking this street this year
so I can hear and see today
this hairy woodpecker tapping away
this fall, da da da dah, da da da dah,
da da da dah, da da da dah, like
an aerial tap dancer, da da da dah,
and then turning his head in the silence
of the hole as if mightily curious,
this woodpecker at the end of this street
tapping away, da da da dah, the fall.

STILL BEFORE SOLSTICE

Sun on somewhat
Riffled water.
From it smoke
Rising and drifting,
Ocean breaking
Lightly, gently.
Smooth sun,
Smooth smoke
Drifting beyond
Merganser-penetrated
Surface smoothness
Near where ocean
Lightly breaks.

AS RAIN BEGINS
AND AUTUMN ENDS

Surf scoters dive like
lawn darts descending
and we

We put on our gear
wet suits and tanks and
lines and all

And over we go
like ducks landing
while above

They pay out and wait until
clad in orange slickers
off they go

Or so it seemed
through glass at
another solstice

EARLY INCENSE

Smoke again, and the sun,
Illumined smoke rising from
Water and sand and bending
South as, peering into water
And smoke, the loon glides north

ARCING AGAIN

As I was reflecting on
The death of pastoralism
I almost missed the manifest of
Mergansers, the diving and skimming,

Those darting silversurface passes,
Those rusty hairs of napes
Expressing life, whatever may
Have happened to the sheep.

AT THE END OF ANOTHER TERM

Sun bright again on smoky water
Tilted gently up to clouds
Ranging low on the horizon

Gulls at this edge of the sea
Stand where water ripples close to
The merganser veeing now through smoke

HALCYON TIME

White on the crown of the scoter
Upright before diving

Broad white patches on the wings
Of the goldeneyes in flight

Heads under wings on the water
Black ducks sleeping
In sight of the kingfisher's wire

AFTER THE THREE DOGS

Dark in the sun near shore, rafting eiders
Carried in and back by brilliance of water
Sometimes breaking over them.

It is not as though they do not drift in light
But always they bob and slide just apart from
The more sustained brilliance

Washing ashore until, more tightly rafting
Now, they bear the light out with them.

SUBSEQUENT TO THE
WOODPECKER VISION

The jay perched in the tree in snow
Exposes to the glasses such a self
As might make one suppose snow
Had made gray docility
Of wagging brashness blue and shrill

But whatever snow has made out there
The black cat sliding on the hood of
The red truck not all that far from
Where the jay was has no reason
To believe in avian transformations

Had it reason it would still not have it
Neither snow nor rain negating flight

IN THE OLD NEIGHBORHOOD

In the bluster of return to cold
In the swirl of new year wind
Crows sail and hang and slide

Inscribe themselves upon the afternoon
That keeps most of us inside

Sociable birds skating the sky
Cawing some but mostly making
New sounds on this cold day

ON EPIPHANY

Having seen again
The merganser's rapier dive
And the broad head and back
And then once more the head of
The seal darkly shining
In January sun

You will settle, will you not,
For the manifestation on
The other pier of only
Two of the graces, especially
Since they're leaving as a centaur,
The new year sun still warm?

AGAIN IN THE PRESENCE OF SUN

The goldeneye dives and dives
Exposing tailfan, tailfan,
Black ducks glide and glide
Not even necks exposing
Paddles. Their element
Rolls and rolls sliding
Its lather in over bristles
Of rocks, stubbles of weed,
Hissing over and over
Whatever it is it says
In its elementary way.

EARLY IN THE DECADE

Standing on rock flattened, streaked, smoothed,
Turned and lined by sand and water, I think
Of granite, the beginning and end of a century,
And as rock doves whirl and buff the air
I hear, though hardly see, waves breaking.
But the veins of these rocks, sanded and unsanded,
How, even now in the absence of sun, brilliant!
How rich even now in the absence of circulation!

And finding myself atop a platform now
For reviewing the swift swimming and diving and now
The low straightnecked flying of a solitary merganser,
I realize that this reviewing is the seeing
Of a bird never seen before, the hearing
Of an utterance never in the garden heard before.

ANDRÉ PROVENÇAL

As baroque waves wash up against
And sometimes over the shaggy backs
Of rocks the scoters move back
And forth in lines and follow into
A circle and to the rocks the rhythm

MIDDLE OF JANUARY SCENE

The sand wears gobs and splashes of gold
But the goldeneye stays out in the water

Mostly diving away from the light
Keeping mostly her back to it

NEAR A DRY MONTH'S ENDING

Goldeneyes, black ducks, gulls
Dive and paddle and peck
And waves swell and break high
While he talks low of Henry and Mary,
Ode and birthday and elegy.

The goldeneyes dive and dive,
The blacks paddle and dabble,
The gulls peck and peck,
All riding it, riding it, riding it
After Henry's playing for Mary.

FEBRUARY MUSIC

The waves of the piano
Rising and falling
In here
      out there
The mergansers and
The goldeneyes
Ride them like notes

RED-BREASTED NUTHATCH

When that stubby tail's
In sight, how is one
To note the line, black
And distinctive,
Going through the eye?

FOR ABE ON HIS DAY

Something not noticed by me before:
The fans of their tails when,
Smooth, the goldeneyes dive. Beyond

Those divers and the black ducks,
Way out, oldsquaws perhaps,
Their quills apparently raised there in

The glasses where, also beyond
The fantails and the dabblers,
Crested heads and razored beaks

Certainly slice air and ocean
While gently on swells the pastel
Tail of the sun floats in and in.

BEFORE ANOTHER READING

Out on the stippled blue
A pair of streaks
Revealed by the glasses as grebes.

What will the glass reveal
The dark circle on
A goosebumped white to be?

MARDI GRAS EARLY AT SEAL COVE

The in close gull and out farther loon
sit on the water ride the morning riffles

From rocks to rocks crows fly in front
avoiding intersection not crossing

The line held fast by loon and gull
even as they drift even as one dives

AFTER THE SEALS

Necks gone with the sun,
The eiders ride squat and plump.
Necks back after rain,
The swan resurrects itself
In the eider once again.

AGAIN AT SEAL COVE

Sun again
Loon again
And in close
Two little divers

Not content
With peering only
They go down
And down again

OFF THE WHITE BEACH

Itching, twitching, waggling,
Looking sometimes when arching
As if calling for a mate,
The preening goldeneye floats through
The snow of early March,
Much of his body now
As usual (even if
Not usually seen as such)
A rather ellipsoid snowball
Corking upon the ocean.

IN BOBOLINK ABSENCE

Light rain pocks the black
newly exposed skin of the pond

Loons and a goldeneye across the way
ride the swelling ocean

And probe below its greenish surface
going from wet above through

Wet below as if there were
A teeming sun to be diving out of

AMONG STARLINGS ON MARCH 9, 1992, IN PORTSMOUTH, NEW HAMPSHIRE

Red-wing blackbirds!

THE PROXY

On St. Patrick's Day
a cardinal in the yard!
Until the advent
of emerald tiara
this prelate
though gone
will do.

ALMOST AT EQUINOX AGAIN

Low again at low tide
the loon cruises low
preparatory to going lower.

Out farther something dark
and something very white
moves neither lower nor higher.

If no loon, what?
Ah, a loon asleep!

BEFORE CLASS

On a drowned day at the edge of
Spring, the river runs out to
The nearby sea, water
Lies in pools on the playing
Fields, a plane ascends,
Gulls soar, branches
Shake in the silent wind,
Shags or geese line
Landwards low against clouds
Sliding seawards. Someone
Walks to the river bank.

MORNING BRIGHT AND BLUE

Where only days ago
ice was
ducks dive

Where no long tails were
days ago
blackbirds perch

But up on the wire
the small hawk
fluffs out her feathers

And down in the marsh
the large fox
continues his rounds

BEFORE THE FLOODING

Though the rain still falls,
Some of the black notes
Are back on their staves
This morning, the first
Of a new month, some
Of them, fidgety,
Sidling, edging and
Edging over on
The wire before scaling
Down to reeds and weeds
On the ground and rocks,
Ice gone from the ponds,
The new water high.

APRIL MORNING READING

Blackbirds swerve and glide
Ruddering selves through morning
Air before inhabiting
Like shades a redbrown bush
Above a pond

        Its
Unshivering black skin
Reflects but does not catch
Probably the pair of gulls
Off on the left manning
Momentarily a chimney

APRIL FRIDAY

for J-P S

Back on his wire the kingfisher,
White and shy waders in the marsh,
Upper branches blooming blackbirds,
Starlings stitching the quilted lawns,
Crows loud as ever in trees,
Tree swallows airing on a wire
Bellies white as sheets on a line,
The tongue budded with sores again.
Existentialism as dead,
They say, as its progenitors.

AFTER THE HAWK

The sun again reveals,
Seals says the rhyme,
But not the glasses and rocks,
Which say, reveal, forms
Of cormorants and gulls.

O sound! How you delight
Us and entice us
As you lead us from view
To view, from view to form,
From form to us to you.

ON GOOD FRIDAY

The loon, knowing what
It's doing, comes up only
Briefly this morning,
Shedding the burden of rain
Under old ocean's surface.

Oblivious of
Heavy rain, driven it seems
By hunger and wings,
The gull ascends and descends
Bearing and dropping darkness.

The man, wrapped within
Glass, encounters the wetness
Of the new morning,
Sees it bead silver and slide
Down the encompassing shield.

APRÈS VOUS

In apparent contrast to
The apparently amicable mergansers
Swimming and diving side by side
The two blackbacked gulls

Were engaged on shore in a tug of war
Over what seemed like the grayish
Remains of a skate. But even they
Seemed after a while to be

Cooperating, for as they yanked
And pulled, the skate seemed
To be splitting just about in the middle, so all
They had to do, I thought,

Was persevere. They persevered
Until the beak of the one
Apparently the stronger lost its purchase
And the other one carried off

The whole torn prize. If you assume
Appearance here was not
Deceiving, what moral would you care
To point? What? That one!

AFTER EASTER

A cormorant in
The pond but no appearance
Of loon in the cove
Until Wolfgang's slow movement
In here resurrects out there
The black head and throat,
The white chest and rest, after
Which one sees, before
They go under, a couple
Of cormorants in the pond.

AND THEN THE PLOVER

Just when one was about to
Bemoan the abundance of light

At a considerable distance
And only on the surface
Briefly before diving again
The loon came into sight

In sight that morning
Black and gray and white
Through abundance of light

IN THE SCRAGGLY BUSHES

The redwing ruffs
fans out his tail
shakes his epaulets
fans and ruffs and before
the drop of a pen

Is gone awol
as if suddenly
deciding
not to wait for
inspection after all

AFTER AN ABSENCE

How easy the loon out there
Makes diving seem. And hard.

The blackblack head dips into
The rippled sandygreen

And almost without a ripple
Is gone as if never there.

AS LIGHT SLICED THIN
ON THE HORIZON

On flexible raft
The eiders roll and ride up
And slide down water
Stringing them out, skeining in,
Sustaining transformation.

AND DOVES OBSERVE

Water left on some of the sand
Shines in the form of candelabra
As blackbirds fly this dull morning

YOUR ANSWER?

Were it not so fierce
Would the kingfisher be
So lovable?

Long-beaked perched intensity,
Ruffled hovering concentration,
Head-first slate-blue purity,
Crested dignity even eating,
Even speckled parts exposing.

AND GULLS

For Roy, apparently not here now

Do eiders always
Hold their necks and heads
Quite so highly arced,
Quite so swanlike, or
Does this morning's light
Uplift them more than
Usual from their
Heavy element?

If I in my machine,
Why not they beyond
Machination?

FOURTH VARIATION

The sea that morning
Was green, sea green except where,
Breaking white and brown,
It hissed in over the sand
To where the gulls were watching.

OR AT 25555

Tail to the withdrawn ocean
A gull lies on the beach.

Out at the mouth of the cove
Lips swell and whiten and

Break over blackened teeth.
The head of the bird turns.

NOT AT BOSHAM

Standing apart and facing the breakers
Two gulls wait for the ocean to come
To them. It having come, they move
Back a bit, these Canutes
Having nothing to prove to a retinue
Though having a poet with something to show
If nothing at all to prove.

ON THE WAY TO A READING

Like occasional notes on a series
Of staves blackbirds perch
On wires until
The notes erased
The wires stretch against
The blue and white expanse of sky

AFTER THE CARDINAL

Beyond the breaking waves
Eiders raft in haze.

Their backs turned, blackbirds
Stand on wires, the white

Ardent sun close now
To penetration.

AND THEN THE TURNSTONES

Eiders dive, their wings
Stuck out almost like rudders
Parallel or fins
Or, better yet, exhaust jets
Of submarine propulsion.

FROM ABOVE AT GRANITE POINT

If he in white and black were not floating
Still beside her there, might not she
Busy dabbling in the ocean edge,
Her above surface form displaying plaits not usually
Seen on her so clear — might not she,
If not he, be an armadillo?

Yes, and yes even with him there —
Except for every now and then that swirl
In air of head emerged, that signature
Of eiderhood down there at the edge.

BEYOND SEAL COVE

In that gray morning the blackbirds on wires
Faced those wavy green slates breaking
Especially white before the reabsorption

FROM NEAR THE TERRITORY

Never more red than
Now in this sun, redwing cleansed
By rain! Never more
Black than set then on that black
Wire for the dive, for the plunge!

MAY DAY AGAIN

The cormorant comes up and flaps heavily
Off. The pair of mergansers, not exactly
Looking like their kind, their bills unnaturally
Long, even for them, come up again.

But when then the male leaps out and down
And in, they have mergansered it again.

AFTER MAY DAY

Nothing that morning
Shone on the ocean
Except the extraordinary
Quotidian white
Of the nape of the gull.

Nothing shone
On or over
The surface of the pond
Except, set
In the water before

A greentrimmed bush
Of russet, black
Chopped limbs of stump
Upholding the peacock
There displayed.

AT ADAMS POINT

We are out on this
breezy sunny Sunday
to get some air
suck up sun
fly kites with the kids

And I out to see birds
think at first
as the wind blows off
the choppy Great Bay
of a silent spring

But approaching the burial mound
and its obelisk
(Reformation John: 1791-1850
topping the list)
I begin to see birds

One and then
a pair of warblers
perched briefly on a branch
and the white of a flicker rump
taking off from grass

And across a pond a kingbird
flying up from
and back to sumac tips
some of the white of his front
splashed on his slate back

And then his mate appears
the slate of her back
unstained by white
her airy dance his
if at some distance

And then from across the bay the great
kingbird of the Air National Guard
lifts and turns back
displaying over water
his stained belly

And making apparently
no more song
than the others
while kites fly
and we walk the breezy point

AS IF OUT OF AFRICA

O ghostly jay
showing at first all breast
how am I to interpret
your pale presence?

Having seen you
manifested before my eyes
like no jay ever
O what am I supposed to say?

If I were to see it
as I have seen you
would I have the courage
as well as the luck?

ON THE BEACH AT FORT FOSTER

Near where the sometimes paired mergansers patrol
a two-or-maybe-somewhat-higher-foot tapering
tower of rocks and a lower non-arched bridge
stand in shades of gray response to the
brown boundary post bearing its
Private Property Thank You
notice and a gray capstone

Ah parody
even here near where
mergansers patrol

Lovely art arcing all the way
back to the age of stone

ACROSS FROM THE SEA

Having hung in air like a bronze Daedalus
The glossy ibis lands at an edge
Of the swamp, near a couple of blackbirds,
And gets to work stitching the mud,
His decurved needle beak and black
Neck undulating out of copper
Shoulders set square as a butt of a loaf
Of new-baked bread, dark bread
Still too hot to touch.

If others work for their bread
his work
one is tempted to say
is inbred
his copper being
not so much earned
as sustaining and sustained
his needlework
completely natural
however artful
he may appear
however far
he may have come
to hang there
over blackbirds

NEAR THE OLD COAST GUARD STATION

Having little, it seems, to say
This sunny morning, the flat
Low-tide waves ripple
Applause of the rippling classical
Music, back-row gulls
Making a somewhat less
Decorous noise. And then

Ah! That dandy, randy
Smell of salt, that
Sharp whiff of quiff!

ONE IN MAY

After the sparrow was struck down
As it flew low across the road,
What was there left to say?
Except, I did not feel any impact
Until, looking in the mirror,
I felt then what I saw.

IN EXAM WEEK

Unlike the eiders
Riding and schooling on the
Sparkling May water
The swallows diving over
It make their own dark sparkling

AFTER A WEDDING

Glistening in the early light
The pair of female eiders glide
Among glistening backs of the woolly
Mammoths of the low-tide shore.

Gliding glistening between glistening
Reflections and rocks, how can these birds
Bear all this early low-tide light?
How can it not turn them too to stone?

BEFORE THE LILACS AND THE MYRTLE

The mowing goes on in South Cemetery
In anticipation of another
Memorial Day and dogwood blooms
Beside the shut up Chapel of
The New Jerusalem and poison
Ivy shines where a bee buzzes over
Both dull and shining leaves at the side
Of the road. Down the road some,
Standing mute and hollow, pining
Polyphemus aims his nose
Not at all directly at
Where, in on the other side,
The congregating crows sing loud.

ACROSS THE RIVER AND IN AND ABOVE IT

While officers and men, standing khaki and blue
On the gray deck above their moored
Submarine, pay their respects to their shipmate
Felled on 4 in a land machine,
US Navy YFN
1204 is tugged past
And the cormorants, one of them gray, converge.

On a wooden deck this side the river
Three women sit while one
Describes her crash and all her scars,
One of them running all the way
From somewhere to her belly button.

AIDED BY THE GLASSES

At the nuns' pond
that forenoon
much life visible:
a couple of cormorants
swimming easily,
noses in the air
as usual;
a pair of warblers
vigorously yellow
in undulant flight;
various other birds
seen in various ways.
But most arresting
the black-crowned heron
apparently set as still
on its rock at the shore
as, somewhat to the left
above and behind it,
showing white through
the green of leaves,
the image of the virgin.

Fabulous orange-eyed stone bird!

There in the daylight
the night heron
suspended in oblivion
of black-crowned imitation of
the white-crowned virgin mother.
Nature and art
art and nature
and supernature
at the nuns' pond
in the morning.

FOLLOWING THE BOBOLINK

Above at low tide, a gull,
Followed by another gull,
A blackbird or two, and then finally,
For a minute or so, four cormorants
Playing black angels. And then

The flowing stage apparently cleared
Again and set for entrance above.

EXPOSURE

Gulls fly over rocks
Exposed at low tide as
Brown and yellowhairy

Ducks swim in gray water
And lobster boats ride
A streak or curl of light

EXCEPT FOR SOUND

Though sounding rough in its ultimate breaking
The water washes smoothly in
Making smoothly rough low ground for
The occasional stridency of gulls.

Eleven female eiders are escorted
By a male across the cove and back
Or the other way around or neither.
Ducks or shags fly low out

Beyond the cove where the haze one sees
The heat to be making seems to be present.
Across the road no haze hangs over
The pond. Smoothness of morning is there.

NEAR SOUTH PLAYGROUND
OVERLOOKING THE COURTS

How on that lower branch
The gray of the kingbird blends in
With the bark of the trees beyond
Until suddenly one sees

It has blended away! But now
On wire or higher branch,
Underparts whitely revealed,
Or in flight, its fringe of tail

Flared white, this bird does not
Blend so. At such heights
One may see both gray
And white, may view up there
Two such kings of the air!

IN AND THROUGH

In the fog the birds flit,
Through it they fly and swim —
Catbird, warbler, blackbird, crow,
Eiders, female and male —
While on rock black-bellied plovers stand.

AGAIN IN THE GARDEN

Hanging from silver chains,
The fern and the fuchsia turn
To and away from each other
Like the gravest of dancers.
Leaves move in the breeze,
Willow and lilac and maple
And, beneath them, those
Of grass, while light and shade
Down there are mostly still.

Coming from some distance,
Traces of barking are,
If not golden, not
Brazen. The sun in the garden
Is warm and the voice of sparrows
Sweet as one brings seeds
To another and the fountain overflows again.

ADAM UNACCOMPANIED

The birds I can do
on my own:
I have herring gull,
bank swallow, catbird,
eider, shag, even
oldsquaw inside me
set for utterance
when movement catches
my eye. But for
doing the flowers,
dear, I need you.
Beyond clover and
daisy and rose I
need you. Even for
morning glory I
have found I need you
for naming, doing.
On this point, in this
familiar eastern
garden, as in that
even more eastern
garden of New Place,
I need your naming,
need your lips and eyes

and all the rest.
Without you, without
me, this point, these birds
and flowers are, but
they no more than I
without you speak. Yes,
even though speaking
began before you.
So even the birds
I now see
I cannot do
on my own.

AFTER CONCORD

The sky above the hill diffused
With streaks, with doves pursued and torn
Apart right there in air, on the wing,
By hawkish birds larger and swifter
Than they, circle and whirl as they may.

In the stands, the crowd roars
Approval of the fireworks display.

You knew and pronounced it good, Ralph Waldo,
You who lost Ellen and Charles
And Waldo, you who hymn throughout
The world the firing behind the manse.

NOT LONG BEFORE THE RAIN

In New Castle harbor,
over waves slapping and
slurping hulls and rocks,
Don Quixote rides again.
A sparrow calls da da da deet,
da da da deet, da da da deet.
Sancho, enchanted, rides
aside and ahead as
the one-master Di Bo.

WALKING IN FROM NEW CASTLE

If one were running, one probably
Would not hear the gulls,
Much less the terns, announcing to
The cormorants the end of
The world, over and over and over.

IN THE MARSH BY BLACKBIRD POND

Perched on beige beads at the end of
A thin green plant a dragonfly,
Staying still there (except for moving
Its head) and holding out steady both
Sets of silver wings edged
And spotted with brown, brings me to wonder
Whether poetry would lose its function,
Like some creature its skin, if only
We knew the names of enough things,
Which is to say, perhaps, if only
Enough of them held obligingly still
Like this dragonfly perched here.

SUNDAY NIGHT AWAY FROM HOME
for Valjeane

Just as if we were at home
We watch the nature program on
The telly while you iron: Where
Something is to be eaten, something
Will come along to eat it, the voice
Says and continues, The food chain here
Is simple: Algae, flamingoes, fish eagles.

Since it breeds in Africa
On volcanic ashes, this is,
I understand, the flamingo as phoenix,
The rare Arabian bird at home.

INSTEAD OF HELVELLYN:
SUNDAY IN GRASMERE

1

Near Allan Bank a thrush with
something in its beak
stands and hops on a wall

Upside down in a gutter
an orange skateboard lies
like a derelict spaceship

Daws chew
finches possess a field
and the first whine of traffic
cuts in

2

At Goody Bridge Farm
water flows steady
like nothing at the shore
as if waves were still to be
unfolded on the earth

Down the sides of a boulder
water falls
like a drooping audible
silver mustache

Like Silenus laughing while
beyond the beck sheep
gaze as if
sound is to be invented

3

In a woods
a robin moves on a path
a nuthatch
warblers and creepers
are active in trees

4

Across from the path where the Rothay rolls
at the edges of a mountain of grass clippings
thrushes and blackbirds are busy
weaving the silence

5

At the entrance to St. Oswald's
wisps of rushes
as if left by birds of air and fields
deck the paving before closed doors

6

From the bench
at the top of the garden
at Dove Cottage
one sees the lake

And fells beyond
and one smells peat
as the sun shines
and it rains a bit

7

In St. Oswald's
rushes smell sweet
and feel soft
underfoot

AT LYMINGTON YACHT HAVEN
WITH THE RAGANS

As this summer evening
Terns cruise and dive
And on the far bank
The gray heron and
The oystercatcher stand,
In the great forest of masts
Halyards slap and slap.

ANNIVERSARY MORNING

What have I learned in all these years?
To see the birds
And the ocean's inroads.

Were there at that beach that morning
Terns, sandpipers,
And low-flying swallows?

If so, I cannot remember
Being aware
Of their moving presence.

What I remember are people
And the weather
And the road back to town.

These are here now as vividly
As plunging terns,
Running pipers,
And low-flying swallows.

AUGUST BEACH

Frisbees now and more people
than years ago when one's bare heels
first made this stretch of sand
pucker and yip, and the women
thinner now and in skimpier suits,
but the same, the one, scene:
the outgoing tide revealing
dark, shaggy rocks and ledges,
ducks and sailboats riding brightness,
their element, and people pretending,
this penultimate Sunday, to be
fixed, bared and whirling, in theirs.

AH THE NAMES OF THINGS

Coming here to the old spot
At an edge of the Big Pond
to look for birds
especially black-crowned night herons
if any remain now that their roosts
are exposed almost to everyone's view

I see plenty of gulls
and the sharp wings of terns
and a pair of kingbirds
mostly perched
and I'm wondering whether

Jacques bird this morning
could have been a glossy ibis
or a green heron
and here I stand among
ferns and plants and bushes
all this green in flower and

I have no name for it
none for them beyond
aster and currant
no name for the marvelous
clustered laces in white and off-white
no name for this jeweled

Profusion of fuzz
these almost orange trumpets
blowing in the breeze
these light mauve quadrants
of tiniest petal
swaying and unfolding at my knees

Ah the work is naming
and one alas hooray
has so few of the names

AUGUST ANNIVERSARY

Female eiders dabbling in breaking waves
Pecking shore birds scuttling among mounds of weeds
Brightness through fog on water and bees among roses

BEFORE THE POETRY CLASS

Over and over
she stands up on the water
shaking her wings
exposing her front

And then she arches
down her head
aparently to peer
and then her back she grooms

Thus the loon
this late summer morning appears
and thus we have to thank
the vermin moving her

IN A GRAY MORNING

Gulls and cormorants, cormorants and catbirds.
In the distance a chainsaw purrs while
In the bushes the catbirds cheep and
Asters stand by the roadside and
White tailfringes by a path
Assert, if not sovereignty,
Kingbird identity if
Not that of cormorant and gull.

STILL

As still as a heron
And its reflection

ALMOST A DECADE AGO

After passing a pair of crows flying
Together to a tree, I thought of monogamy.

When I came to a pair of squirrels squashed
On the road in parallel, steering between

I thought of fidelity, who might as well
Have confronted mobility. But then seaducks

Swimming into the sun in line brought back,
For no apparent reason, monogamy.

MILL POND TRIO

Swimming in and going under almost
At their golden feet, the cormorant taunting
The pair of egrets is really poaching, one sees,

As it comes up with something wiggling in
Its beak. But then, one reflects, such distinction
Cannot be meaningful to those two white ones standing

And darting empty beaked on the green shore.
But then when those beaks come up with wiggling things,
The underwater swimmer is revealed as

Beater. And if one stayed there looking longer?
But one, of course, has not their natural patience.

BRIEFLY ON THE BEACH

Scampering back and forth and pecking in
The water washing them back and forth, how
Deliberate, how conscious are those plovers
Of the sources of their movements? Do

They see themselves stabbing at themselves
As well as into what is under? Do
They ever wonder, or is it all
As instinctive as their plumpness? Or

If not so entirely, reflective only
Superficially? And we? Though we
Reflect in ways apparently not
Available to them, do we see

Ourselves reflecting in the surface of
The element in and which they dance?
See us pecking there controlled like them
By tides? As we seek to colonize

Above both sea and birds, we do well
To see their natural innocence, brute
Beauty, do well to see brutal grace
In this necessity we threaten, cannot

Deserve, must love, do well to see
The elements washing, moving, dancing them,
The very air and earth, the fire and water
Moving us all upon these visible shores.

BEHIND THE MUSEUM ON THE
LAST SUNDAY

The ocean being
Tilted up to intersect
The sky, no wonder
The cormorants stand on rock,
Stand looking, looking, looking.

SOUTH MILL POND DANCE

In the nearly empty mill pond
Against the gray of stinking mud
Again extensively exposed
The white of five snowy egrets

Until rather green legs, lifted,
Bring to light feet ungilded by
Yellow slippers. And then appear,

In the slice of water in which
They feed, five more white forms moving
As those over them are moving,
Five white forms lifting beaks meeting

Beaks descending, five forms wading,
Skittering, standing, and jabbing
Skittering, standing, and jabbing
White forms moving above them there.

As green legs and absent slippers
Transpose those snowy egrets in-
To little blue herons, young and
White in immature plumage, so

In that foul muck first five and then
Ten forms expose their fair selves
Dancing there their lovely white dance,

Five forms first and then ten, and then,
Startled and air-born, five again.

STARTING IN HURRICANE SEASON

Seen by the eye unaided, peeps
Running and pecking at the edge of the sea
Seem small, dark, scampering things.

Seen by the aided eye, they wear
Grays and whites and brown, they are
Plovers charged with aggressive beauty.

Seen by eye of memory,
Plovers prance at the edge of the sea
Like horses, like plump, black-bellied steeds.

A NOTE ON "INSTEAD OF HELVELLYN"

Helvellyn, a dominant mountain north of Grasmere, in the Lake District of England, is an important presence in William Wordsworth's poetry. Book VIII of *The Prelude*, for instance, begins with a substantial section devoted to presenting the sounds and sights of the annual Grasmere Fair as they are heard and seen by "Old Helvellyn."

Though Wordsworth climbed Helvellyn often, doing it once even with the lame Sir Walter Scott, I, having less love of heights than some, passed up an opportunity one Sunday to climb Helvellyn. Choosing instead a more domestic route, I strolled around the town that Wordsworth in 1799 chose as his actual and symbolic home.

William and Dorothy Wordsworth, and later William's wife Mary and their children, lived first in Grasmere at what came to be known as Dove Cottage. When in 1808 the size of the family necessitated a removal from that former inn at Town's End, the Wordsworths did not settle immediately at Rydal Mount, where they were destined to live for the rest of William's long life (1770-1850). Instead, they moved first to a large new house called Allan Bank and then in 1811 they moved to the rectory across the street from Grasmere's parish church, St. Oswald's, living there until, in 1813, they moved to Rydal.

So for more than three years the Wordsworth children, sometimes joined by those of Coleridge, had at Allan Bank extensive grounds for roaming and playing in. And the adult males too, Wordsworth and Coleridge and, often, De Quincey and Southey, had plenty of room for walking as they talked politics and poetry on paths just a bit west of Grasmere village.

Dove Cottage and Rydal Mount are both these days open to those of the public willing to pay the entrance fees. Though The Rectory and Allan Bank are not open to the public, one can still walk near them, can pass The Rectory on one side as St. Oswald's goes by on the other, can walk the avenue to Allan Bank and then move past the house by following the old path to the right.

Bearing new rushes for spreading on the floor of the local church was once a regular action embedded in the liturgical year in England (and, no doubt, elsewhere). One of the few places in which this custom from medieval times survives is Grasmere, where new rushes are, one Saturday afternoon each summer, borne in festive procession through the streets of the town to St. Oswald's Church, the graveyard of which contains what is left of the bodies of, among others, William, Dorothy, and Mary Wordsworth.

Banners as well as rushes are borne in the procession. The following lines may give readers who have not themselves seen the Grasmere rushbearing some idea of how, one Sunday, the soft, sweet-smelling rushes actually go to be in, and just outside the main door of, St. Oswald's:

LEVAVI OCULOS
CANTATE DOMINO

HOPE RULES A LAND FOREVER GREEN

Children in green and white
Leading old people
Followed by the head shepherd
Vested in white and red

The Ulverton Band plays
The bells of St. Oswald's sing
Bing, Bam, Bong

Bystanders hear and see and are moved

140

ABOUT THE AUTHOR

Though he has traveled beyond his native region, especially in Ireland and England, by birth and inclination Hugh Hennedy is a New Englander. After living at Biddeford Pool, Maine, for about twenty-five years, he has moved to Portsmouth, New Hampshire.

A graduate of Notre Dame, Columbia, and Boston universities, Hennedy taught at the University of New England in Biddeford, where he is Professor Emeritus.

He has published essays on Chaucer, Shakespeare, and Austen and a book on Trollope, *Unity in Barsetshire* (The Hague, 1971). His first collection of poems, *Old Winchester Hill*, appeared in May, 1993 (Enright House of Ireland). His poems have appeared in a number of journals including *Puckerbrush Review*, *Tar River Poetry*, and *Roanoke Review*.

AND THE ILLUSTRATOR

Charles Chu taught Chinese at the Monterey Language School and Yale University, and from 1965 to his retirement at Connecticut College, where he chaired the Chinese department and now is Curator of the Chu-Griffiths Art Collection. Other books he has illustrated include *Edged in Light* by Jane Jordan (1993) and *Grace Unfolding* by Greg Johansen (1991).

Other Books from the Oyster River Press

Edged in Light. Poems by Jane Baymore Jordan. Illustrated by
  Charles Chu. 1993. 1 882291 52 2

Intense Experience. Social Psychology through Poetry. 1990.
  Fred Samuels. Ed. 0 9617481 6 8

Is It Poison Ivy? by Joan Raysor Darlington, author & illustrator.
  1993. 1 882291 53 0

A Letter to My Daughter, 1687, by the Marquis of Halifax. With
Essays from a New England College Town (1927-1987). P. Taylor.
  1992. 0 9617481 4 1

The Mending of the Sky and other Chinese Myths. Retold by
  Xiao Ming Li. Illus. Shan Ming Wu. 1989. 09617481 33

Ombres et Soleil Sun and Shadows. Poems and prose by
  Paul Eluard, 1913-1952. Illus. Picasso, Chagall, Magritte,
  others. 1993. 0 9617481 7 6

Peace in Exile. Poems by David Oates. 1992. 0 9617481 9 2

Thoughts for the Free Life. Lao Tsu to the Present. 2nd ed. 1989.
  P. Taylor. Ed. Illus. 0 9617481 5 X